TELL ME MORE! science

BATS

by Ruth Owen

Ruby Tuesday Books

Published in 2021 by Ruby Tuesday Books Ltd.

Designer: Emma Randall
Editor: Mark J. Sachner
Production: John Lingham

Photo credits:
Alamy: 18; FLPA: 4, 7, 8–9, 13, 22 (top left); Nature Picture Library: 6, 10, 12, 14–15, 19, 20–21; Science Photo Library: 17; Shutterstock: Cover, 1, 5, 11, 16, 22 (top right), 22 (bottom), 23.

Library of Congress Control Number: 2020946809
Print (hardback) ISBN 978-1-78856-171-6
Print (paperback) ISBN 978-1-78856-172-3
eBook ISBN 978-1-78856-173-0

Printed and published in the United States of America
For further information including rights and permissions requests, please contact: **shan@rubytuesdaybooks.com**
Reprinted 2023

Contents

Is It a Bird? Is It a Plane?

No! It's a small, furry animal called a bat.

Bats aren't birds—they are **mammals**.

There are more than 1,400 different kinds of bats.

They are the only mammals that can fly.

Honduran white bat

Let's Talk

What things do all mammals have in common?

(The answer is on page 24.)

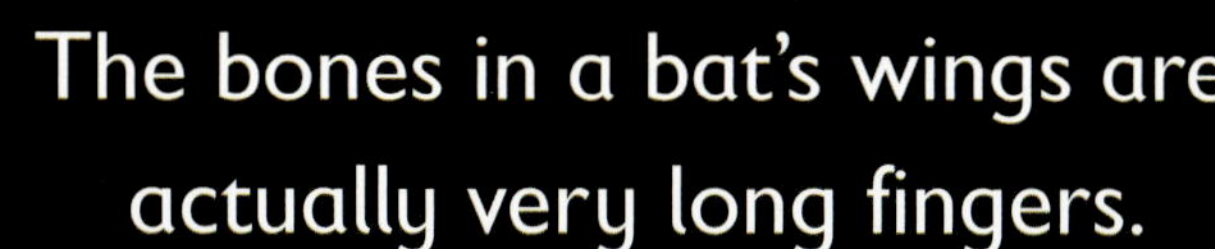

The bones in a bat's wings are actually very long fingers.

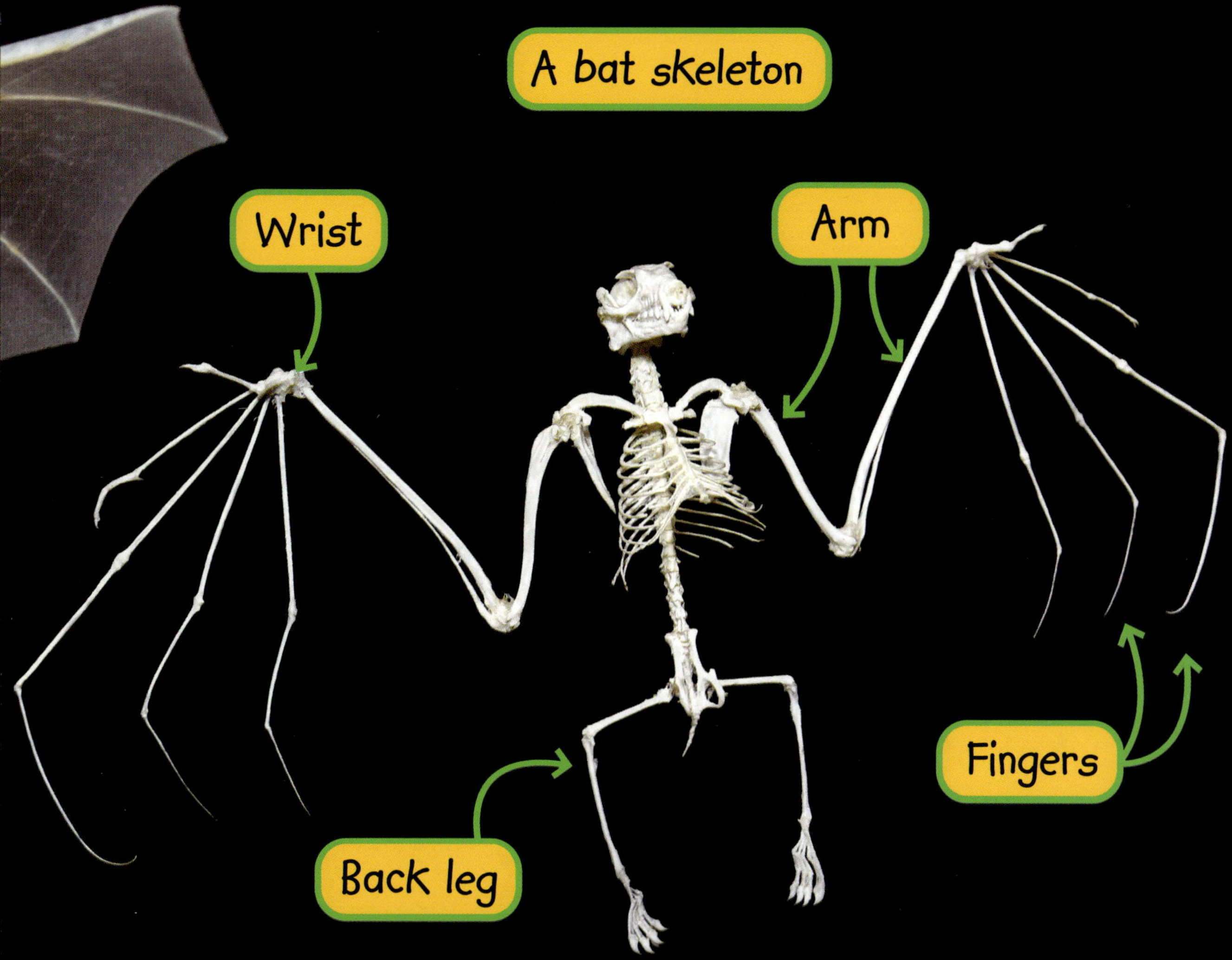

A bat skeleton

Wrist

Arm

Fingers

Back leg

The biggest bats are flying fox bats. Some kinds have a **wingspan** of up to 6 feet (2 m). The bumblebee bat is the smallest. It weighs less than a dime.

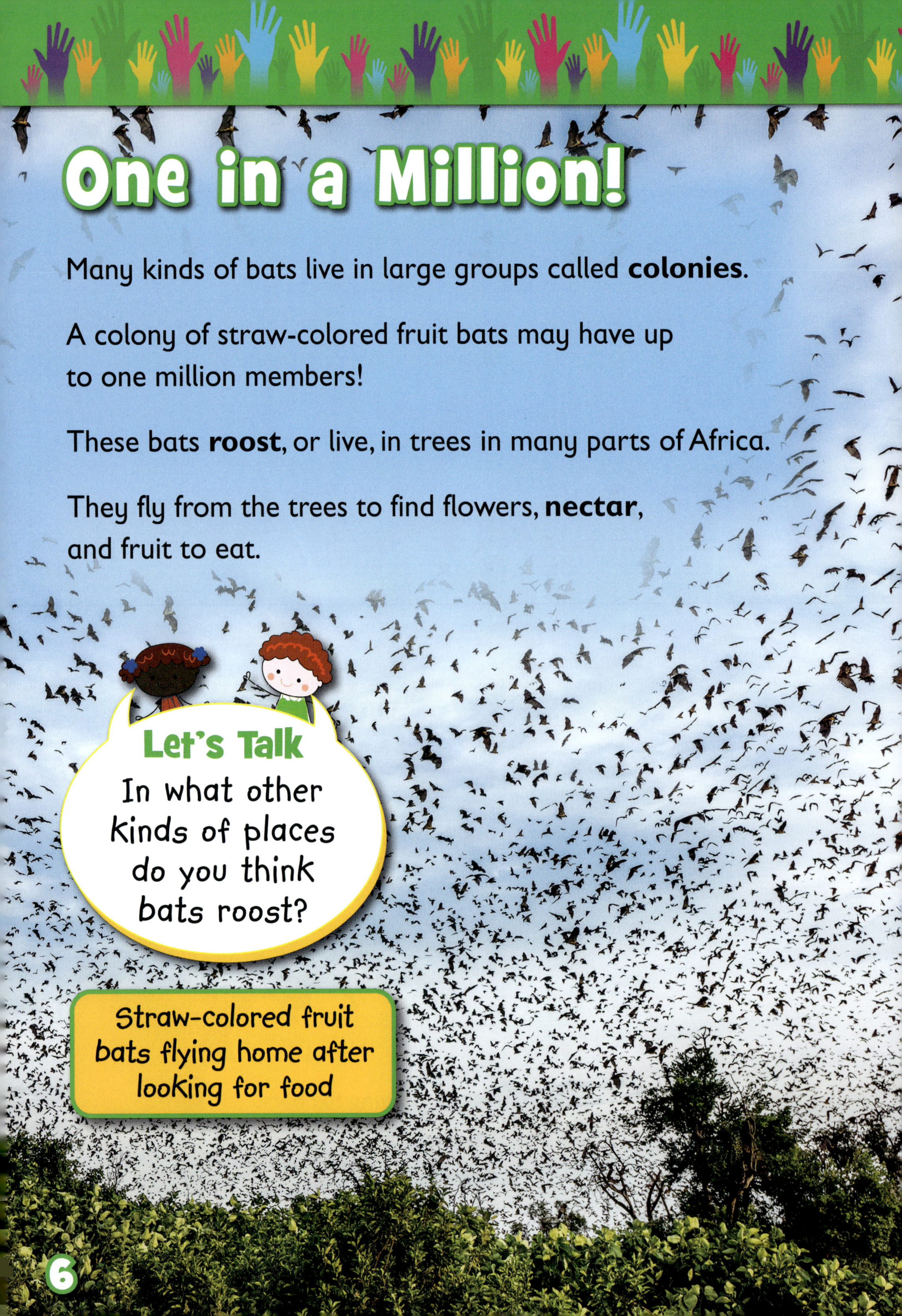

One in a Million!

Many kinds of bats live in large groups called **colonies**.

A colony of straw-colored fruit bats may have up to one million members!

These bats **roost**, or live, in trees in many parts of Africa.

They fly from the trees to find flowers, **nectar**, and fruit to eat.

Let's Talk

In what other kinds of places do you think bats roost?

Straw-colored fruit bats flying home after looking for food

When bats are roosting, they hang upside-down by their feet. Hanging in this way helps them take off. When it's time to fly, they let go, start to fall, and then whoosh—they're off!

Home Sweet Home

Some bats roost in caves or hollow trees.

Others live in old buildings and roof spaces in houses.

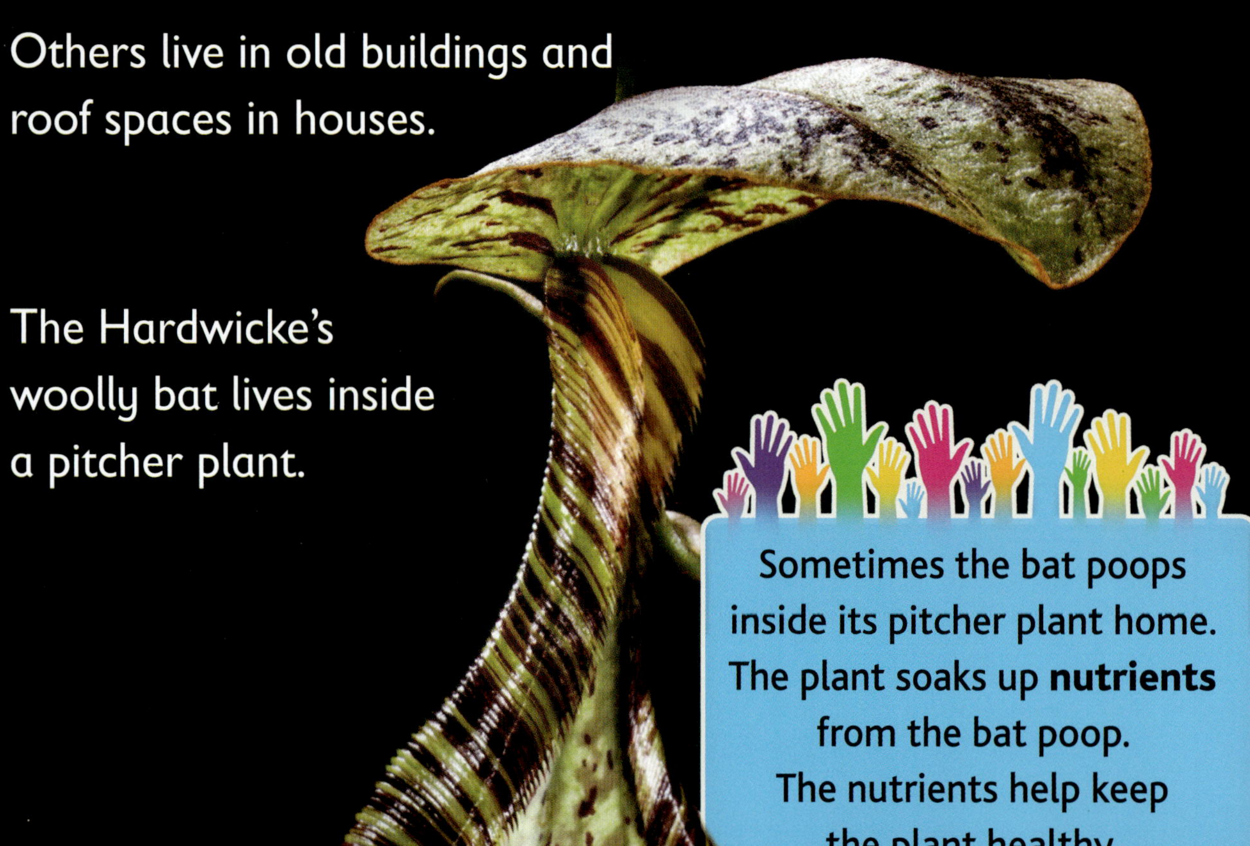

The Hardwicke's woolly bat lives inside a pitcher plant.

Sometimes the bat poops inside its pitcher plant home. The plant soaks up **nutrients** from the bat poop. The nutrients help keep the plant healthy.

The Madagascar sucker-footed bat roosts inside a rolled-up leaf.

It has tiny pads on its wrists and ankles that release a sticky liquid.

The sucker-footed bat roosts right way up.

The liquid attaches the bat to its leaf home.

A Bat Goes Hunting

Many types of bats use a system called **echolocation** to hunt for flying insects.

As a bat flies, it makes shouting sounds.

The sounds bounce off an insect and return to the bat as **echoes**.

The echoes give the bat information about the insect's location, or position.

Then the bat gives chase!

Some bats have a part on their face called a nose leaf. It helps focus the bat's echolocation sounds. The greater horseshoe bat gets its name from its horseshoe-shaped nose leaf.

More Hungry Bats

The fringe-lipped bat's favorite food is frogs!

This 4-inch- (10-cm-) long flying predator also eats small lizards and large insects, such as beetles.

A fringe-lipped bat

The Cuban flower bat leaves its cave at night to find flowers.

Then it feeds on seeds and dusty **pollen**.

Let's Talk

Why do you think seed-eating bats are helpful to plants?

A Cuban flower bat inside a flower

A flower needs pollen from another flower to help it make seeds. As a Cuban flower bat feeds, pollen sticks to its furry body. Then it carries the pollen from flower to flower.

Helpful Bat Poop

A fruit bat is eating juicy figs and the seeds inside.

Then, as it flies from tree to tree—plop!

Some bat poop falls to the forest floor.

Inside the poop are seeds that have passed through the bat's body.

The bat has just helped a fig tree spread its seeds to a new growing place.

The bat poop around the seeds will help them grow into new plants. That's because the poop contains lots of nutrients.

Fig seeds

Tiny Vampires

For the tiny vampire bat there's only one thing on the menu—blood!

At night, a vampire bat flies from its cave.

It looks for a sleeping cow, horse, bird, or other animal.

Then the bat bites its **prey** with its sharp **fangs**.

As blood oozes from the wound, the bat licks it up.

Vampire bat

Vampire bats live in large colonies. Sometimes a bat can't find a meal. Then another member of the colony that has fed will spit up some blood for its hungry neighbor.

Moms and Pups

When female bats are ready to give birth, they roost together in a **maternity** colony.

Most mother bats give birth to just one pup.

The tiny baby feeds on milk from its mother's body.

A scientist holds a mother Egyptian fruit bat

When a mother bat goes hunting or looking for food, her baby goes too. The pup holds on tight with its feet and teeth!

Some types of bat pups cling to their moms for about four to six weeks.

Then they are ready to learn to fly and find food.

Others stay with their moms for longer.

Bat Rescue

Sometimes bat moms get sick or injured, and they die.

At the Tolga bat hospital in Australia, **volunteers** take care of pups that have lost their moms.

Spectacled flying fox pup

The volunteers feed the pups with milk from a tiny bottle or syringe.

When the pups are about two months old, they are also fed fruit.

Once the pups can fly and find their own food, they are released back into the forest.

Be a Bat Scientist

Scientists who study animals carefully watch them to learn about their behavior. Observe the bat behavior in these photos and try to answer the questions. (The answers are on page 24.)

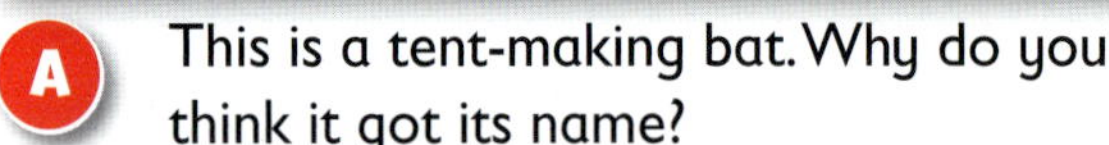

A This is a tent-making bat. Why do you think it got its name?

B What do you think this bat is doing?

C What kind of food do you think this bat is eating?

Guess the Bat Number

1. Bats are fast flyers. What's the fastest flying speed that scientists have measured?
2. How many insects can a bat catch in one night by using echolocation?
3. How many types of plants need help from bats to make seeds?

(The answers are at the bottom of the page.)

Answers:

1) The Brazilian free-flying bat at 100 miles per hour (160 km/h) 2) 3,000 insects
3) 500 plants, including banana and mango trees

Glossary

colony
A large group of animals that lives together.

echo
A sound that returns to where it came from after bouncing off of a hard surface.

echolocation
A system in which an animal makes a sound that bounces back off an object and then returns to the animal as an echo.

fang
A long, sharp tooth.

mammal
A warm-blooded animal with hair or fur. Mammals give birth to live babies and feed them milk.

maternity
Having to do with being pregnant and giving birth to babies.

nectar
A sweet, sugary liquid produced by flowers that insects, bats, birds, and other animals eat.

nutrients
Substances that are needed by living things to help them grow and stay healthy.

pollen
A colored dust that is made by flowers and is needed for making seeds.

prey
An animal that is hunted by other animals for food.

roost
To settle in a place to rest or sleep. "Roost" is also the word for a bat's home.

volunteer
A person who does work for an organization without being paid.

wingspan
The measurement of an animal's wings from wingtip to wingtip.

Honduran white bats roosting in a leaf tent

Markovics, Joyce. *Little Brown Bats (In Winter, Where Do They Go?)* Minneapolis, MN: Bearport Publishing (2015).

Owen, Ruth. *Wings, Paws, Scales, and Claws: Let's Investigate Animal Bodies (Get Started With STEM)*. Minneapolis, MN: Ruby Tuesday Books (2017).

Answers

Page 4:

All mammals have hair or fur. They have a backbone and other bones in their bodies. Mammals are warm-blooded. This means they are able to generate their own body heat. Mammals breathe air with body parts called lungs. Female mammals give birth to live babies and feed them milk from their bodies.

Page 22:

A) Tent-making bats got their name because they roost in tents made from leaves. The bats bite at a leaf so it folds in half and makes a shelter that's shaped like an upside-down V.

B) The bat has visited a pond for a drink. As a bat flies over a pond or lake, it swoops down and scoops up a mouthful of water.

C) The orange nectar bat in the picture is using its tongue to feed on nectar from the flower.